NATIONAL GEOGRAPHIC KiDS

weird but true! 2

2

350 OUTRAGEOUS FACTS

NATIONAL GEOGRAPHIC
WASHINGTON, D.C.

A bottlenose dolphin has a bigger brain than a human.

Snow leopards can't roar.

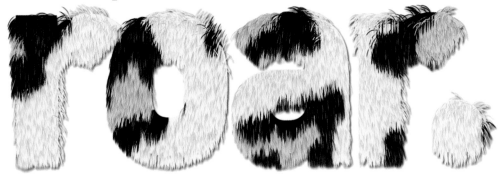

A BRITISH JEWELER MADE A TEA BAG DECORATED WITH 280 DIAMONDS—IT WAS WORTH £7,500! (ABOUT $12,000)

ONLY FEMALE BEES STING.

If you continued to **grow** as fast as an average baby, you'd weigh about **413,300 pounds** by age 10. (187,470 kg)

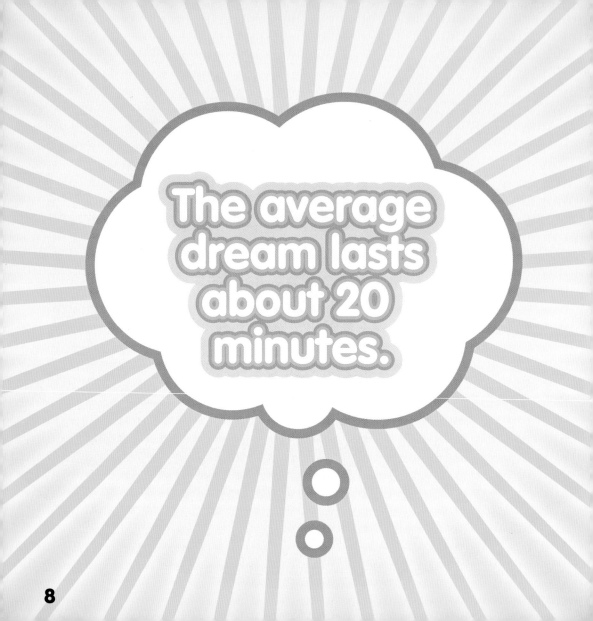

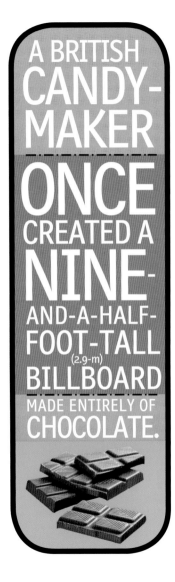

A BRITISH CANDY-MAKER ONCE CREATED A NINE-AND-A-HALF-FOOT-TALL (2.9-m) BILLBOARD MADE ENTIRELY OF CHOCOLATE.

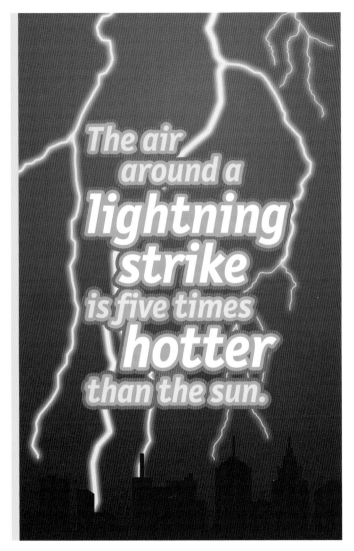

The air around a **lightning** *strike* is five times **hotter** than the sun.

9

Some avalanches travel more than 100 miles an hour.

(161 km/h)

A HUMAN BONE IS FIVE TIMES STRONGER THAN A PIECE OF STEEL OF THE SAME WEIGHT.

THE LONGEST RAW EGG TOSS WAS 150 YARDS. (137 m)

100 YARDS (91 m) LONG

THE DOTS ON DICE ARE CALLED PIPS.

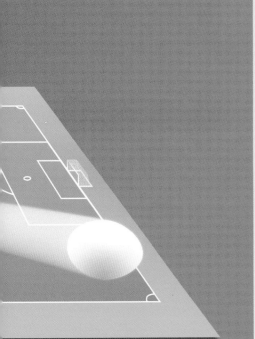

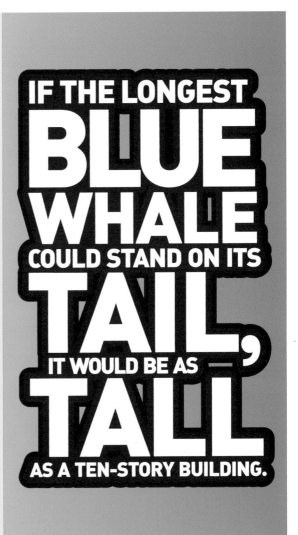

IF THE LONGEST BLUE WHALE COULD STAND ON ITS TAIL, IT WOULD BE AS TALL AS A TEN-STORY BUILDING.

Bats have thumbs.

ROCKETS MUST TRAVEL

AT LEAST 25,000 MILES AN HOUR
(40,234 km/h)

TO ESCAPE EARTH'S GRAVITY.

There have been at least four major ice ages.

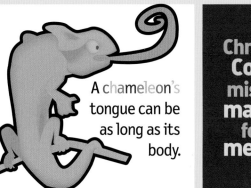

A chameleon's tongue can be as long as its body.

Christopher **Columbus** mistook a **manatee** for a **mermaid.**

Light **travels *faster* than sound.**

A newborn puppy can take up to **two** months to start wagging its tail.

Popcorn can pop up to three feet into the
(0.9 m)
air.

The **London Bridge** that kept **falling down** is now in Arizona, in the United States.

A *ZEPTOSECOND* IS ONE-BILLIONTH OF A TRILLIONTH OF A SECOND.

NOTHING CAN ESCAPE FROM A BLACK HOLE.

AN AMERICAN MAN COOKED 427 OMELETS IN 30 MINUTES.

Some butterflies' **ears** are on their **wings.**

Fingernails grow faster than toenails.

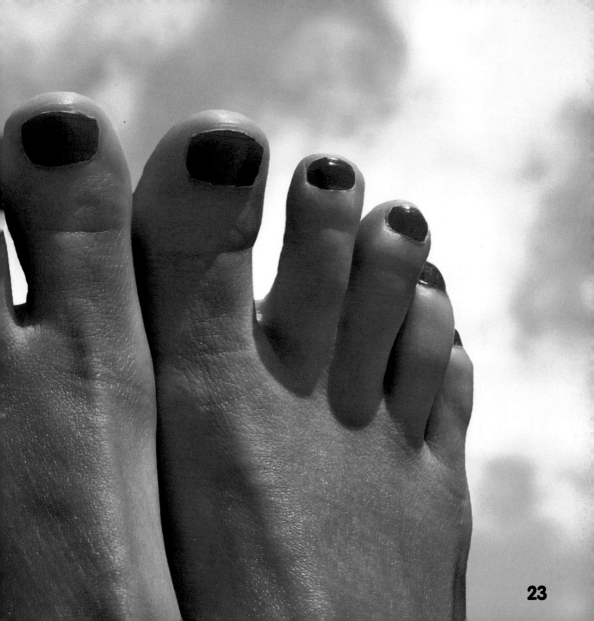

23

A camel can drink 500 cups (118 L) of water in ten minutes.

Gelotology is the study of laughter.

A supermarket in South Africa created a pizza that was 122 feet 8 inches across *(37.4 m) and weighed as much as two male African elephants.

IF YOU TRAVELED AT THE SPEED OF LIGHT, YOU COULD REACH PLUTO IN JUST FOUR HOURS.

SOME FROGS GLOW WHEN THEY EAT FIREFLIES.

MEN GET THE HICCUPS MORE OFTEN THAN WOMEN DO.

A *JIFFY* is one-hundredth of a second.

THE WORLD'S TALLEST WATERFALL, CALLED **ANGEL FALLS,** IS **TALLER** THAN **FIVE** WASHINGTON MONUMENTS STACKED UP.

YOU ARE MADE UP OF ABOUT 10 TRILLION CELLS.

CHEWING **GUM** was banned in Singapore until 2004.

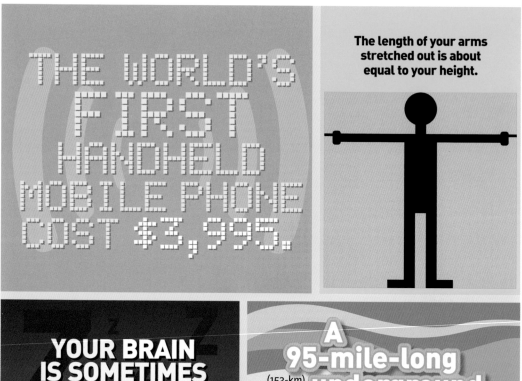

THE WORLD'S FIRST HANDHELD MOBILE PHONE COST $3,995.

The length of your arms stretched out is about equal to your height.

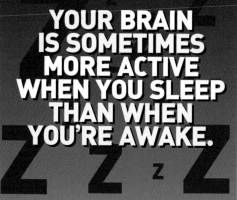

YOUR BRAIN IS SOMETIMES MORE ACTIVE WHEN YOU SLEEP THAN WHEN YOU'RE AWAKE.

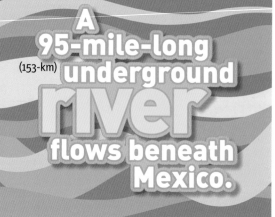

A 95-mile-long (153-km) underground river flows beneath Mexico.

Americans eat 1.2 billion pounds (544 million kg) of potato chips a year—more than ten times the weight of Egypt's Great Pyramid.

DINOSAUR BONES WERE MISTAKEN FOR DRAGON BONES WHEN THEY WERE DISCOVERED MORE THAN 2,000 YEARS AGO.

NEWBORN BABIES ARE
COLOR-BLIND.

A 5,000-year-old piece of chewing gum was discovered in Finland.

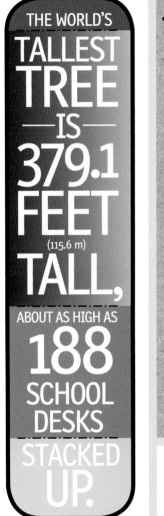

THE WORLD'S **TALLEST TREE IS 379.1 FEET** (115.6 m) **TALL,** ABOUT AS HIGH AS **188 SCHOOL DESKS** STACKED UP.

A PIECE OF **CAKE** MORE THAN **4,000** YEARS OLD WAS FOUND IN A **TOMB** IN EGYPT.

MALE MOSQUITOES DON'T BITE.

One year on Neptune lasts about 165 Earth years.

ASTRONAUT **NEIL** ARMSTRONG LEFT HIS **SPACE BOOTS** ON THE **MOON.**

THE **FIRST** MICROWAVE **OVEN** WAS ALMOST AS **TALL** AS A REFRIGERATOR.

Some spiders eat their own webs.

There are about 16 million

thunderstorms
on Earth
every year.

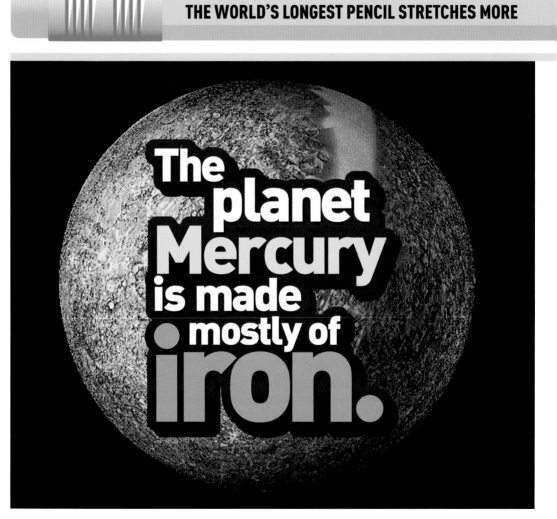

The planet Mercury is made mostly of iron.

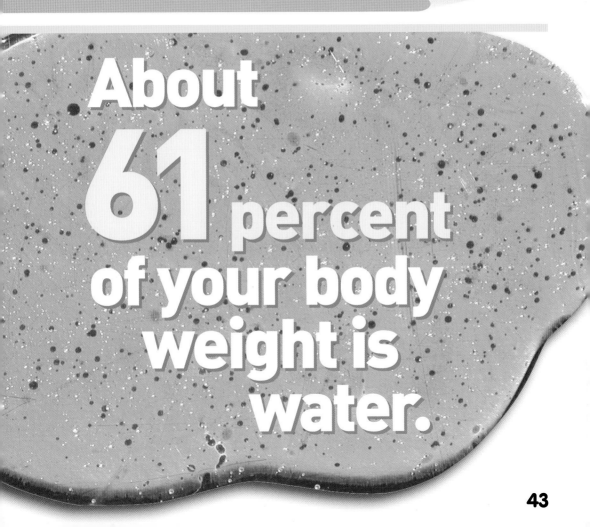

About **61** percent of your body weight is water.

PANAMANIAN GOLDEN FROGS catch the attention of a mate by sitting on a riverbank and waving.

A METEORITE SCULPTED TO LOOK LIKE A **CHICKEN SANDWICH** sold for **$20,000.**

Until the mid-1800s, there was **NO DIFFERENCE BETWEEN LEFT AND RIGHT SHOES.**

The **ICEBERG** hit by the *TITANIC* is thought to have been about **100,000** years old.

PREHISTORIC *QUETZALCOATLUS,* THE WORLD'S **LARGEST FLYING REPTILE,** HAD THE WINGSPAN OF A SMALL AIRPLANE.

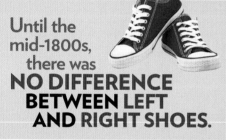

A **250-ACRE** (100-ha) solar energy farm in **CHINA** is shaped like **Giant Pandas.**

A RAT'S NOSTRILS SMELL independently of each other.

PENGUINS are attracted to the smell of **ROTTEN EGGS.**

BUS STOPS in **KONAGAI, JAPAN, ARE SHAPED LIKE FRUIT.**

HERMIT CRABS use their LARGE LEFT CLAW for defense and their SMALL RIGHT CLAW to collect and eat food.

That's Weird!

You can buy **GLOW-IN-THE-DARK DOUGHNUTS** at a BAKERY in AUSTRALIA.

HORSES can make more **FACIAL EXPRESSIONS** than **CHIMPS** and **DOGS.**

THE HEARTS
OF SOME
HUMMINGBIRDS
CAN BEAT MORE THAN

1,000

TIMES A MINUTE.

The ancient Aztec used cacao (cocoa) beans as money.

Rhinoceroses don't sweat.

A hill in New Zealand is named Taumatawhakatangihangakoauauo

IT'S POSSIBLE TO SMELL SCENTS IN DREAMS.

tamateapokaiwhenuakitanatahu.

THE GREAT BARRIER REEF

IN AUSTRALIA IS THE BIGGEST LIVING STRUCTURE ON EARTH.

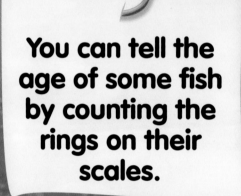

You can tell the age of some fish by counting the rings on their scales.

Bloodhounds can follow a scent that is **four** **days old.**

THE **SUN** IS **93** MILLION MILES AWAY.

(150 million km)

MOST OF TODAY'S

CALCULATORS

ARE MORE POWERFUL THAN THE WORLD'S FIRST COMPUTER.

ANIMALS THAT LAY EGGS DON'T HAVE BELLY BUTTONS.

A tiger's stripes are different on the left and right sides of its body.

The **first email** was **sent** in **1971.**

RUSSIA IS ONLY TWO MILES FROM ALASKA.
(3.2 km)

A GROUP OF BLUE JAYS IS CALLED A PARTY.

There are more than **250,000 different words** in the English language.

SHARKS HAVE NO BONES.

CATS CAN'T TASTE SWEETS.

Some robots can identify different cheeses.

A COCKROACH CAN LIVE FOR OVER A **WEEK** WITHOUT A HEAD.

Earth's core is about the same size as the planet **Mars.**

Thousands of tiny earthquakes happen every day.

THE SAHARA DESERT IS LARGER THAN AUSTRALIA.

Venus is the hottest planet in our solar system.

LIONS SPEND ABOUT 20 HOURS A DAY RESTING.

A **TIGER** can eat more than **80** pounds (36 kg) of meat in one sitting.

Most **people** spend about **five years** of their **lives** eating.

A HIPPO CAN RUN AS FAST AS A HUMAN.

A man **hiccuped** for 68 years straight.

METEORITES THE SIZE OF BASKETBALLS LAND ON EARTH ABOUT ONCE A MONTH.

NIGHTTIME RAINBOWS ARE CALLED MOONBOWS.

Enough whipped topping is manufactured every year to crisscross the United States more than 5 times.

75% of all animals are insects.

THE WINGSPAN OF A **747** IS **LONGER** THAN THE **WRIGHT BROTHERS'** **FIRST FLIGHT.**

SCIENTISTS KNOW MORE ABOUT THE SURFACE OF **THE MOON** THAN THE BOTTOM OF **THE OCEAN.**

Engineers reversed the flow of the Chicago River.

ON SUNNY DAYS, THE **EIFFEL TOWER** IN **PARIS, FRANCE, LEANS TOWARD THE SHADE.**

Crocodiles can't chew.

65

A dog can make about

100

different facial expressions.

The
Earth
is slightly
pear-
shaped.

A zebra's skin is black; only its fur is striped.

A TROPICAL **ANT** CAN SNAP ITS JAWS TOGETHER AT A SPEED OF 145 MILES AN HOUR, (233 km/h) FASTER THAN ANY OTHER ANIMAL!

69

It takes the average 10-year-old kid

about 20 minutes to fall asleep.

MOUNT EVEREST GROWS MORE THAN ONE-EIGHTH OF AN INCH (3 mm) EACH YEAR.

1/8 inch

0mm
10
20
30
40

1

2

"Old man" is a nickname for a male **kangaroo.**

One million seconds **is 11** days, **13** hours, 46 minutes, and 40 seconds.

The brighter the star, the **shorter** its life span.

French fries came from

Belgium, not France.

GRAVITY PULLS UP, DOWN, AND SIDEWAYS AT THE CENTER OF THE EARTH.

THERE ARE MORE TV SETS IN THE UNITED STATES THAN THERE ARE PEOPLE IN THE UNITED KINGDOM.

WHEN YOU SEE LIGHTNING, IT'S TRAVELING AT ABOUT 227 MILLION MILES AN HOUR. (365 million km/h)

A **volcano** in Italy has been erupting for 2,000 years.

TURTLES LIVED ON EARTH BEFORE DINOSAURS DID.

Queen Margherita of Savoy ordered the first pizza delivery in 1889.

The
oldest
valentine
in existence
was written
in 1415.

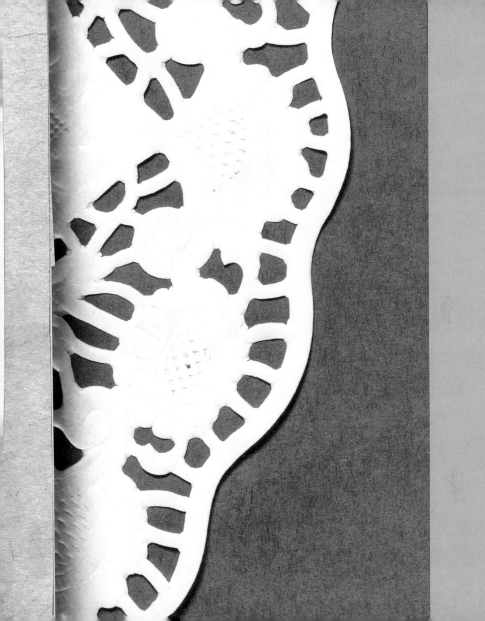

Dalmatians are born without spots.

GIRAFFES WERE ONCE CALLED CAMELOPARDS BECAUSE PEOPLE THOUGHT THEY WERE HALF CAMEL ~AND~ HALF LEOPARD.

THERE IS NO SOUND IN SPACE.

Of any animal, the **pig** has a **diet** most like a human's.

Couples in Finland can get married in a chapel built out of snow.

Some **chickens** lay **green** or **blue eggs.**

You take about **25,000 breaths** every day.

The longest a person has gone without **sleep** is ten days.

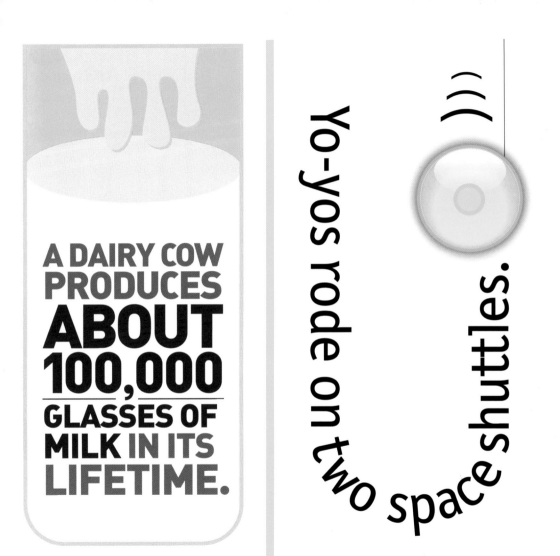

A DAIRY COW PRODUCES ABOUT 100,000 GLASSES OF MILK IN ITS LIFETIME.

Yo-yos rode on two space shuttles.

MEENAKSHI AMMAN, a Hindu temple in India, CONTAINS AN ESTIMATED **33,000** SCULPTURES.

YOU CAN LEARN PROFESSIONAL ACROBATIC and **CIRCUS ACTS** at a clown college in Illinois, U.S.A.

11 of the 12 ASTRONAUTS who walked on the moon had been **BOY SCOUTS.**

Archaeologists recently found a **3,700-YEAR-OLD** CERAMIC JUG with a **SMILEY FACE** painted on it.

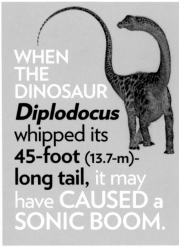

WHEN THE DINOSAUR *Diplodocus* whipped its **45-foot** (13.7-m)-**long tail,** it may have **CAUSED a SONIC BOOM.**

During medieval times, **HAIR BALLS** were used as an **ANTIDOTE TO POISONS.**

The **Floating Instrument Platform (FLIP)** is designed to ROTATE A FULL 90 DEGREES in the ocean for underwater research.

In Spanish, *ARMADILLO* means **"LITTLE ARMORED ONE."**

For more than **100** years, the **IOWA STATE FAIR** has commissioned a **COW SCULPTURE** made from **600** POUNDS of **BUTTER.** (272 kg)

There was once a **BEAVER POND** where **NEW YORK CITY'S TIMES SQUARE** currently stands.

FEMALE MOUNTAIN GOATS are called **NANNIES.**

That's Weird!

KOALAS STAY AWAKE FOR ONLY FOUR HOURS A DAY.

EELS CAN SW

IT IS IMPOSSIBLE TO SNEEZE WITH YOUR EYES OPEN.

The **PRAYING MANTIS** is the only insect that can **LOOK OVER ITS SHOULDER.**

JUPITER HAS 63 MOONS.

Stretched out, your **digestive system** is nearly **30 feet long.**

(9.5 m)

Apples are one-quarter air.

Babies yawn before they are born.

Scents smell better through your

right nostril

than your left.

A GROUP OF PORCUPINES IS CALLED A PRICKLE.

Eating shrimp can turn white flamingos pink.

The average person **walks** about **80,000 miles** (128,750 km) in a lifetime.

That's more than three times around the world!

The **NORTH POLE** is **warmer than** the **SOUTH POLE.**

CATERPILLARS
have mouths, but
BUTTERFLIES
don't.

Earth
is the only planet
not named after a
**Greek or
Roman god.**

You can tell lions apart by the spots at the base of their whiskers.

Hippopotomonstros

Bees visit about
five million flowers
to make one average-size jar of honey.

esquippedaliophobia
is the fear of long words.

Recycling one soda can a TV for three hours.

saves enough energy to run

Only **MALE TOADS**

Croak.

A man **flung a coin** more than ten feet using his **earlobe as a slingshot.** (3 m)

Your tongue grows new **taste buds** about every two weeks.

THE BAHAMAS ONCE HAD AN UNDERSEA POST OFFICE.

The world's **biggest frog** IS THE SIZE OF A house cat.

The total **earthworm** population in the **United States** **weighs** ten times **more** than the total human population.

A **porcupine** can have 30,000 quills.

One **ear of corn** has about **500** kernels.

GIRAFFES
are one of the only animals born with horns.

Wearing a hat on your head helps warm your feet.

All cats are born with **blue eyes.**

MONKEYS CAN GO **BALD** IN OLD AGE, JUST LIKE **HUMANS** CAN.

SIX MILLION POUNDS OF (2.7 million kg) **SPACE DUST** SETTLE ON EARTH EVERY YEAR.

A 3,000-YEAR-OLD MUMMY CAN STILL HAVE **FINGERPRINTS.**

A **snowflake** can take up to **two hours** to fall from a **cloud** to the ground.

PUMPKINS ALSO COME IN

RED, GREEN, YELLOW, BLUE, TAN & WHITE.

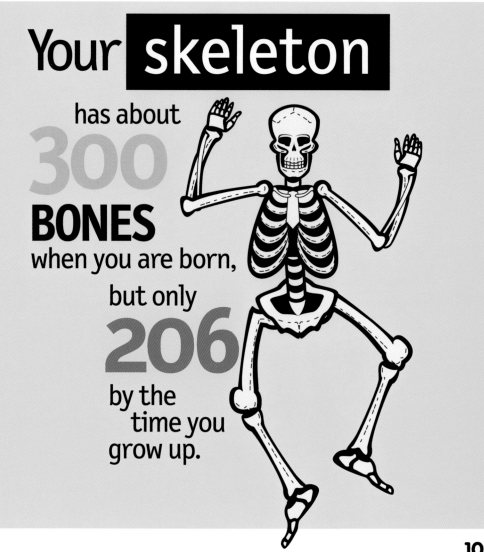

Your skeleton has about **300 BONES** when you are born, but only **206** by the time you grow up.

An ostrich's eye is bigger than its brain.

LINED UP END TO END, ALL THE HARRY POTTER BOOKS SOLD COULD CIRCLE THE EARTH MORE THAN TWICE.

TARANTULAS CAN LIVE FOR UP TO 20 YEARS.

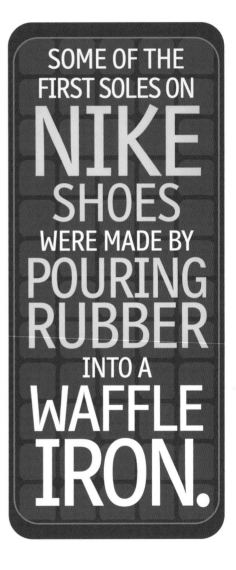

SOME OF THE FIRST SOLES ON NIKE SHOES WERE MADE BY POURING RUBBER INTO A WAFFLE IRON.

The Earth's temperature rises slightly **during a full moon.**

A Rubik's Cube can make
43,252,003,274,489,856,000
different **combinations.**

Popsicles WERE INVENTED BY AN **11-year-old.**

AN OSTRICH CAN RUN AS FAST AS A RACEHORSE.

Sharks have existed LONGER than trees.

ONE (5 mL) TEASPOON OF SEAWATER CONTAINS FIVE MILLION LIVING ORGANISMS.

From about **March 21** to September 23 the **sun never sets** at the **North Pole.**

SOME WORMS CAN GROW

Scientists found a 4,000-year-old "lunch box" in the Bernese Alps.

Winter lasts for 21 years on Uranus.

TO 100 FEET LONG.
(31 m)

Most **squid** have three hearts.

ASTRONAUTS **GROW** — UP TO — 3 INCHES
(7.6 cm)
TALLER IN OUTER **SPACE**.

Jupiter weighs
twice as MUCH
as all the other planets
in our
solar system
combined.

ABOUT

75

PERCENT

OF ALL

VOLCANOES

ARE

UNDERWATER.

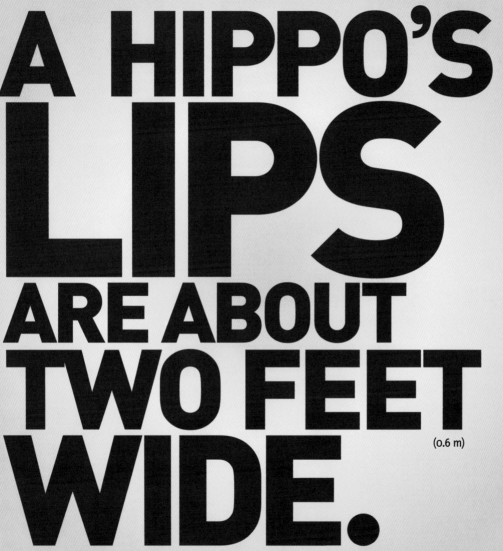

A HIPPO'S LIPS ARE ABOUT TWO FEET WIDE. (0.6 m)

GIGANTIC JETS
=
LIGHTNING THAT **SHOOTS UP FROM CLOUDS** INTO THE ATMOSPHERE INSTEAD OF **DOWN TO EARTH**

Tourists throw more than **one million** DOLLARS into **ROME, ITALY'S TREVI FOUNTAIN** every year.

RAVENS roll around in the **SNOW.**

Professional tennis players **GRUNT** at a higher pitch **when they are LOSING A GAME** than when they are winning, a study found.

DOCTORS RECENTLY FOUND **27** CONTACT LENSES LOST IN A **woman's eye.**

You can stay in a **CABIN** in the **SHAPE OF AN OWL** in southwest France.

The **PUPILS** of an ORIENTAL FIRE-BELLIED **TOAD** are shaped like **TRIANGLES.**

TORTOISES can **FEEL** when their **SHELLS ARE BEING TOUCHED.**

Some **SPIDERS** have ABDOMENS that look like **DISCO BALLS**.

A BAG USED TO COLLECT ROCKS ON THE MOON during the Apollo 11 mission **SOLD AT AN AUCTION** for **$1.8 MILLION.**

LUNAR SAMPLE RETURN

IN RUSSIA, it is considered **BAD LUCK** to **SHAKE HANDS** in the **THRESHOLD** of a **DOORWAY.**

Thieves in ENGLAND recently stole **88 POUNDS** (40 kg) of prize-winning **cheddar cheese.**

That's Weird! •••

FAIRY-WREN BIRDS teach their UNHATCHED CHICKS a **"PASSWORD"** to keep other birds from sneaking into the nest.

SOUTH AFRICA'S GIANT BULLFROG SOMETIMES ATTACKS LIONS.

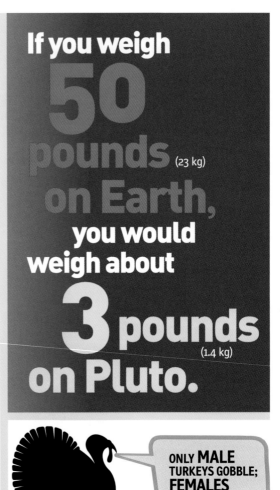

If you weigh **50 pounds** (23 kg) on Earth, you would weigh about **3 pounds** (1.4 kg) on Pluto.

ONLY **MALE TURKEYS GOBBLE; FEMALES CLICK.**

It would take about

788,832,000

two-inch yellow
(5-cm)
sticky notes

to encircle the globe.

OYSTERS CHANGE FROM MALE TO FEMALE.

A space suit costs about ten million dollars.

elephants

Without clothes, you would start to **feel cold** at **77°F.**

(25°C)

The world's first **underwater hotel** is in Key Largo, Florida, U.S.A.

can use their trunks as snorkels.

Fish can't close their eyes.

Detached
sea star
arms
sometimes grow
new >>>>
bodies.

Your eyes produce a teaspoon of tears every hour. (5 mL)

When you have lived for **2.4 billion seconds,** you will be **75 years old.**

Originally carrots were **purple,** not orange.

1,000,000,000,000,000 (that's one quadrillion) **ants** live on Earth.

8,962 people made snow angels at the **same** time on the grounds of the North Dakota State Capitol in the U.S.A.

The flag of every **country** in the world has at least one of the five colors in the **Olympic rings:** blue, yellow, **black**, green, and **red**.

HAWAII IS MOVING ABOUT THREE INCHES CLOSER TO JAPAN EVERY YEAR.

(7.6 cm)

About **150,000 hairs** are growing on your head **right now.**

Geckos can *break off* their own tails.

A litter of kittens is also called a **kindle.**

Some fish have natural antifreeze in their blood.

HUMANS AND SLUGS SHARE MORE THAN HALF OF THEIR GENES.

Alligators' eggs hatch male babies in hot temperatures and female babies in cooler temperatures.

Astronomers have discovered a star that is made of a 10-billion-trillion-trillion-carat diamond.

A head of **broccoli** is made up of **hundreds of small flower buds.**

A storm
on Neptune was as wide as ...

the entire
Earth.

Chewing **gum** can make your heart beat **faster.**

A 158-year-old **holiday card** was auctioned off in the U.K. for nearly **£22,250** (about $35,000).

The **surface** of the Atlantic Ocean is **saltier** than the surface of the **Pacific Ocean.**

The
**50 tallest
mountains**
in the world
are all in
Asia.

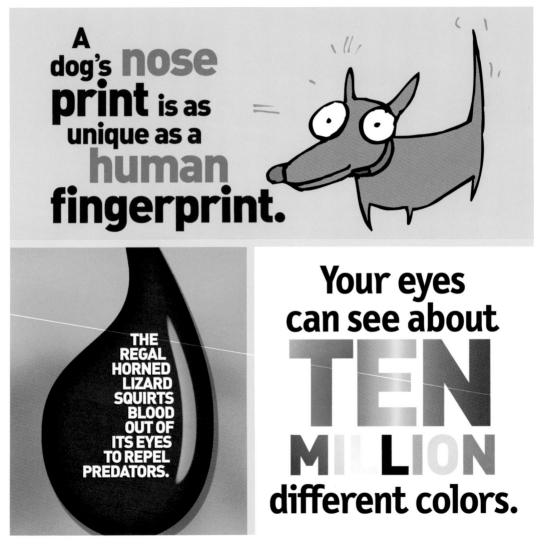

A dog's **nose print** is as unique as a **human** fingerprint.

THE REGAL HORNED LIZARD SQUIRTS BLOOD OUT OF ITS EYES TO REPEL PREDATORS.

Your eyes can see about **TEN MILLION** different colors.

Didaskaleinophobia

is the fear of going to school.

The **lowest known temperature** on Earth **(-128.6°F)** (-89.2°C) was recorded in **Antarctica.**

Ancient Egyptians took up to **70 days** to make a **mummy.**

BEFORE TOOTHPASTE WAS INVENTED, SOME PEOPLE CLEANED THEIR TEETH WITH **CHARCOAL.**

The **Great Wall of China** spans roughly **4,500 miles—** (7,240 km) that's almost as long as the continent of **Africa.**

URP!

SHEEP BURPS CONTRIBUTE TO GLOBAL WARMING.

The heaviest known lobster weighed **44.6** (20.2 kg) **pounds.**

September begins on the same day of the week as **December every year.**

A WOMAN IN CALIFORNIA, U.S.A., REMEMBERS ALMOST EVERY DAY OF HER LIFE ...

SINCE SHE WAS 11.

Tyrannosaurus rex means "tyrant lizard king" in Latin.

GRRR!

The
sun
has enough
energy
to burn
for
100 billion
more years.

A **swordfish** can swim ...

about as fast as a cheetah can run.

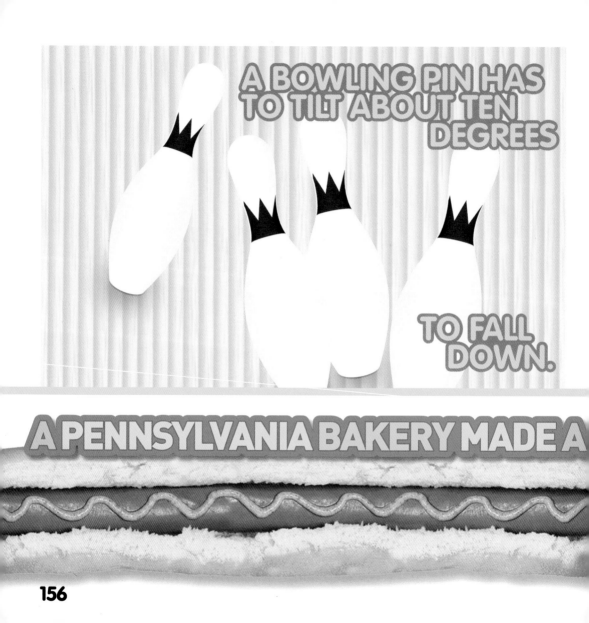

A BOWLING PIN HAS TO TILT ABOUT TEN DEGREES

TO FALL DOWN.

A PENNSYLVANIA BAKERY MADE A

The hottest stars are blue.

SCIENTISTS BELIEVE THAT SATURN'S RINGS WILL EVENTUALLY DISAPPEAR.

HOT DOG THAT WAS 54 FEET LONG.
(16 m)

It would take a stack of **more than nine Empire State Buildings** to equal the average depth of the ocean.

The **"barking pigeon"** has a call that sounds like a **loud dog.**

SAND melts at around **3000°F.**

(1649°C)

ALL OF TODAY'S PET HAMSTERS CAN BE TRACED BACK TO **ONE HAMSTER FAMILY** THAT LIVED IN **SYRIA** IN 1930.

A HOUSE CAT'S TOP SPEED IS ABOUT

31 MILES AN HOUR.
(50 km/h)

The largest **spider** in the world is wider than a **basketball.**

An average of about **353,000** people are **born** every day.

The oldest bat fossil ever found was **50 million years old.**

When **bald eagles** were named, the word **"bald"** meant **"white."**

There is real **GOLD** in the sun.

Humans **blink** about **17,000 times a day.**

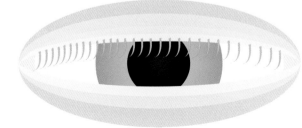

GLASS CAN LAST FOR MILLIONS OF YEARS ON EARTH.

THE LONGEST GAME OF MONOPOLY PLAYED IN A TREE HOUSE LASTED **286** HOURS.

Some **giant jellyfish** have **tentacles** that could **stretch** more than the length of a **basketball court.**

Groups of **SPERM WHALES** sometimes **SLEEP VERTICALLY** (straight up and down).

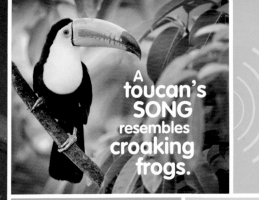

A **toucan's SONG** resembles **croaking frogs.**

The **BRAIN WAVES** between two people **SYNC** when they are in conversation.

A **SUBWAY CAR** in Taipei City, Taiwan, was recently **DECORATED** to look like a **SWIMMING POOL.**

The Mars rover **CURIOSITY** played the song **"HAPPY BIRTHDAY TO YOU"** to mark the first anniversary of its landing.

The **BIBLIO-MAT** is a **VENDING MACHINE** in Toronto, Canada, that **DISPENSES BOOKS.**

Some **CATERPILLARS** live in tunnels inside leaves.

A woman won **$10,000** for a **WEDDING DRESS** she made out of toilet paper.

A study found that **HEAT** makes **PEOPLE MEANER.**

The average **AMERICAN** eats **45 PINTS** (21 L) of **ICE CREAM PER YEAR.**

BEES are more likely to land on a painting that **features FLOWERS** than **still-life** paintings, researchers found.

SCIENTISTS have created **ONIONS THAT DON'T MAKE YOU CRY** when cutting them.

BABIES can recognize the **DIFFERENCE** between **LANGUAGES** before they're **BORN.**

BABY HEDGEHOGS are called **HOGLETS.**

That's Weird!

About 12,000 animal crackers are created every minute.

About one-tenth of the Earth's surface is covered in ice.

Houseflies buzz in

A QUICK-HANDED **PERFORMER** **TWISTED** **747** BALLOON SCULPTURES IN **1** HOUR.

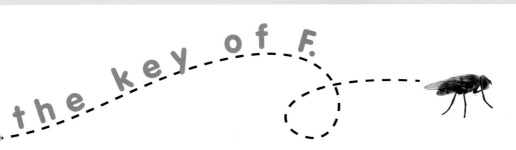

the key of F.

The **air** trapped inside an **iceberg** can be **thousands of years old.**

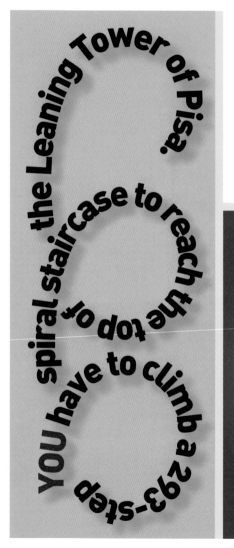

You have to climb a 293-step spiral staircase to reach the top of the Leaning Tower of Pisa.

Chickens
see daylight
45 minutes
before humans do.

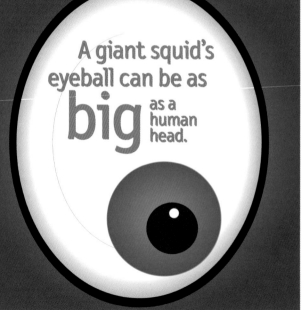

A giant squid's eyeball can be as **big** as a human head.

There's a **one in a trillion** chance that a piece of **space junk** will land on your house today.

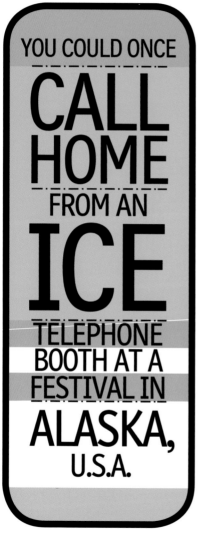

YOU COULD ONCE **CALL HOME** FROM AN **ICE** TELEPHONE BOOTH AT A FESTIVAL IN **ALASKA,** U.S.A.

THE WORLD'S TINIEST SEAHORSE IS SMALLER THAN A POSTAGE STAMP.

THE LARGEST **HURRICANES** CAN MEASURE **TEN MILES** (16 km) **FROM TOP TO BOTTOM.**

The largest salamanders can grow as long as bicycles.

A Canadian juice company made a 195-gallon (738-L) fruit smoothie that could have filled four bathtubs.

175

Apes laugh when tickled.

If you spent a **dollar** every second, it would take about **32 years** to spend a **billion dollars.**

176

An octopus can have nearly **2,000 suckers** on its arms.

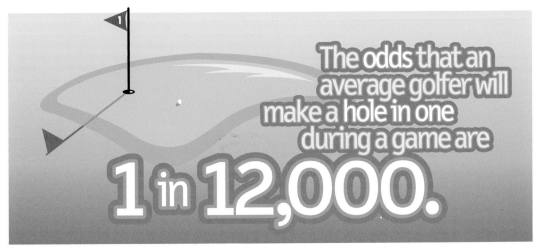

The odds that an average golfer will make a hole in one during a game are **1 in 12,000.**

177

Earth travels about **1.6 MILLION MILES** (2.6 million km) every day.

AN ALLIGATOR GROWS ABOUT **3,000 TEETH** IN A LIFETIME.

MANATEES ARE RELATED TO *ELEPHANTS.*

A 14-pound
(6.4-kg)
pearl was found
in a giant
clam.

Rubber bands last longer when refrigerated.

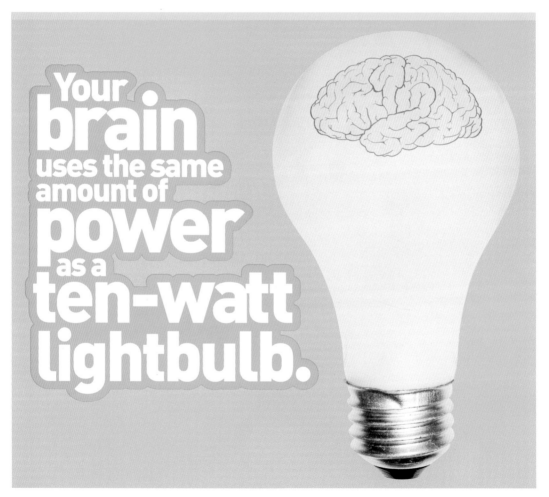

Your **brain** uses the same amount of **power** as a **ten-watt lightbulb.**

THERE ARE MORE TEXT MESSAGES SENT EACH DAY THAN THERE ARE PEOPLE ON EARTH.

A **cornflake** shaped like the U.S. state of Illinois sold for **$1,350.**

Saturn is made partly of **helium**—the same gas used to fill party balloons.

Most pirates never buried their loot.

A gold nugget found in California, U.S.A., weighed a whopping 160 pounds—about as much as 12 bowling balls.

(72.6 kg)

Kangaroos lick their forearms to stay cool.

Your **ears** produce more **wax** when you're **afraid.**

YOUR **HEARTBEAT** IS SO POWERFUL THAT IT COULD SHOOT WATER SIX FEET (1.8 m) INTO THE AIR.

Nomads created **ice skates** made of **bone** at least **4,000 years ago.**

The **Queen** of **England** has a **crown studded** with more than **3,000** precious gems.

A *Tyrannosaurus* rex fossil was sold to a museum for more than eight million dollars.

The binturong, a southeast Asian mammal, smells like buttered popcorn when excited.

A snake can **eat prey** that is **twice the width** of its head.

A cave in Croatia has a 1,683-foot-deep pit—the (513-m) **deepest hole on Earth.**

A group of sea otters is called a raft.

The offspring of a whale and a dolphin is a **wholphin.**

650 HOUSE-FLIES weigh less than **ONE OUNCE.** (28 g)

A rattlesnake's **rattle** is made of the same material as your fingernails.

A mouse's heart is shorter than a Tic Tac.

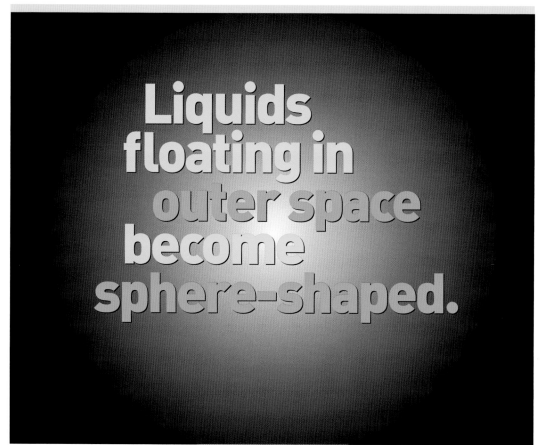

Liquids floating in outer space become sphere-shaped.

A seahorse can move its eyes in opposite directions.

A HUMAN EYELASH LASTS APPROXIMATELY THREE TO FIVE MONTHS.

197

An eagle can spot a rabbit from more than a mile away.

(1.6 km)

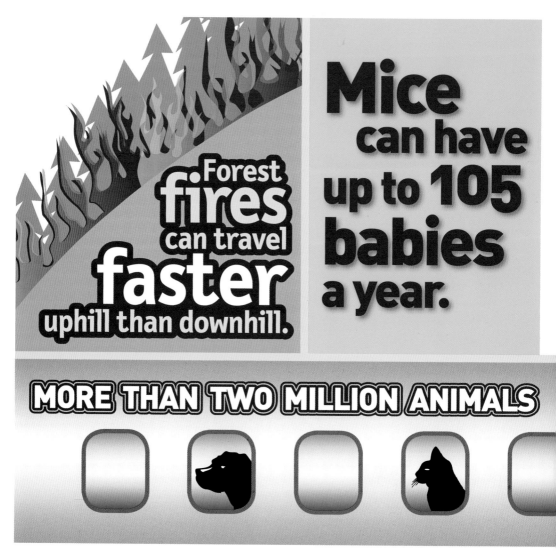

Forest **fires** can travel **faster** uphill than downhill.

Mice can have up to **105** babies a year.

MORE THAN TWO MILLION ANIMALS

A **sandcastle** in Maine, U.S.A., stood as **high** as a three-story building.

FLY IN AIRPLANES EVERY YEAR.

Peaches and almonds are related.

A **56**-LEAF CLOVER WAS DISCOVERED IN **JAPAN.**

A **red flag** was a symbol for **battle** in ancient **Rome.**

A **newborn koala** is about the size of a **jelly bean.**

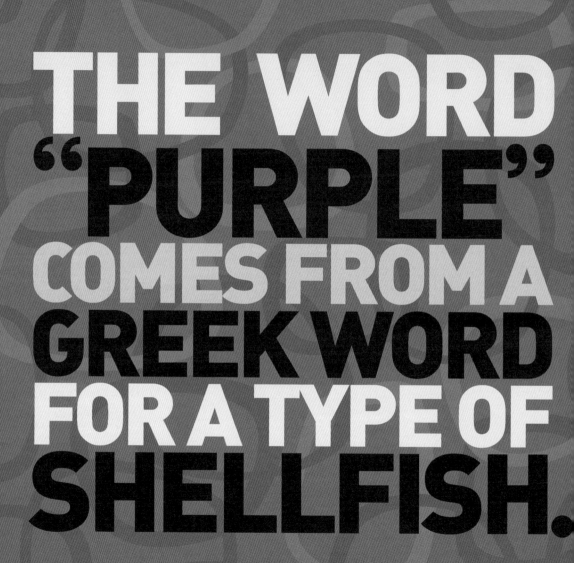

THE WORD "PURPLE" COMES FROM A GREEK WORD FOR A TYPE OF SHELLFISH.

The highest known **jump** by a **pig** is 27.5 inches— (69.9 cm) that's the height of a St. Bernard!

GUESS
WHAT?

Every day you lose 100 of these!
WHAT?

A lizard sticks out its tongue at you!
WHY?

WANNA
FIND OUT?

Spit can freeze in midair here!
WHERE?

The FUN doesn't have to end here! Find these far-out facts and more in *Weird But True! 3*.

Weird but true! 3
350 OUTRAGEOUS FACTS

NATIONAL GEOGRAPHIC KiDS

FACTFINDER

Boldface indicates illustrations.

FACTFINDER

FACTFINDER

PHOTOCREDITS

Cover: (zebra), Suzi Eszterhas/Minden Pictures; **spine:** (zebra), vblinov/Shutterstock; 2, Suzi Eszterhas/Minden Pictures; 4-5, Digital Vision; 6, SuperStock; 9, Maram/Shutterstock; 10-11, Tom Bean/Getty Images; 13, Jonathan Halling; 16-17, Martin Valigursky/iStockphoto.com; 21, George Grall/National Geographic Creative; 22-23, Sam Sefton/iStockphoto.com; 25, Lew Robertson/Getty Images; 26, Friedrich Saurer/Photo Researchers, Inc.; 27, Tushchakorn/Shutterstock; 28-29, Edgar Quintero/National Geographic Creative; 30, Sebastian Kaulitzki/iStockphoto.com; 31, Corbin Halling; 33, Jonathan Halling; 34-35, Franco Tempesta; 40-41, Zajac David/National Geographic Creative; 42, USGS/Photo Researchers, Inc; 44 (UP LE), Miles Barton/NPL/Minden Pictures; 44 (UP RT), Romolo Tavani/Shutterstock; 44 (CTR LE), Preto Perola/Shutterstock; 44 (CTR RT), Stocktrek Images/National Geographic Creative; 44 (LO LE), VCG/Getty Images; 45 (UP LE), javarman/Shutterstock; 45 (UP RT), 2017 John S Lander/Getty Images; 45 (LO), Inara Prusakova/Offset; 46, Stan Osolinski/Getty Images; 48-49, Debra James/Shutterstock; 50, JPL-Caltech/NASA; 53, Rolf Nussbaumer/naturepl.com; 60-61, Tom Brakefield/Corbis/Getty Images; 63, Tobik/Shutterstock; 66, Digital Vision; 69, Digital Vision; 72-73, Aleksandr Stennikov/iStockphoto.com; 75, Donna Castle/National Geographic Creative;78-79, Mark Thiessen, NGP; 84 (UP LE), Michal Knitl/Shutterstock; 84 (UP CTR), Stocktrek Images/National Geographic Creative; 84 (RT), Hong Li/Shutterstock; 84 (LO LE), Denis Poroy/AP/REX/Shutterstock; 84 (LO RT), Denis Poroy/AP/REX/Shutterstock; 85 (UP LE), Eric Isselee/Shutterstock; 85 (UP RT), Luciano Mortula - LGM/Shutterstock; 85 (LO), Zoran Karapancev/Shutterstock; 87, John Carnemolla/iStockphoto.com; 88, iStockphoto.com; 92-93, Digital Vision; 98, Olga Lis/Shutterstock; 99, Shutterstock; 104-105, Jochen Sand/Digital Vision/Getty Images; 110-111, Michael Nichols/National Geographic Creative; 116-117, Anouk Stricher/iStockphoto.com; 122, Eric Isselée/Shutterstock; 124 (UP LE), Elka Liot & Grégory Foulard Muscapix; 124 (UP RT), Leonard Zhukovsky/Shutterstock; 124 (CTR LE), Angela N Perryman/Shutterstock; 124 (LO LE), Mongkolchon Akesin/Shutterstock; 124 (LO CTR), Viktor Loki/Shutterstock; 124 (LO CTR), Viktor Loki/Shutterstock; 124 (LO RT), Svetoslav Radkov/Shutterstock; 125 (UP LE), AP/REX/Shutterstock; 125 (UP RT), Nicky Bay; 125 (LO), Steven David Miller/NPL/Minden Pictures; 130-131, Martin Strmko/iStockphoto.com; 136-137, Lise Gagne/iStockphoto.com; 139, Chris Johns/National Geographic Creative; 140, Ryasick Photography/Shutterstock; 142, NASA; 143, NASA; 145, Kim Bardoel/National Geographic Creative; 148-149, James L. Stanfield/National Geographic Creative; 150, Digital Vision/PunchStock; 151 (LE), Simple Stock Shots; 151 (CTR), Rubberball/Jupiterimages; 151 (RT), Joe Atlas/Brand X Pictures/Jupiterimages; 152, Jonathan Halling; 154, Brian Skerry/National Geographic Creative; 155, Chris Johns/National Geographic Creative; 158 (UP), Jonathan Halling; 158, JD/ARDEA; 159 (RT), Jonathan Halling; 159 (LE), Jane Burton/naturepl.com; 159, Redmond Durrell/Alamy; 160-161, Martin Lukasiewicz/National Geographic Creative; 162, Jonathan Halling; 164 (UP LE), Flip Nicklin/Minden Pictures; 164 (UP RT), Ondrej Prosicky/Shutterstock; 164 (CTR), Ruth Black/Shutterstock; 164 (LO), Carlo Allegri/Reuters; 165 (UP CTR), iShift/Shutterstock; 165 (UP LE), Kelenart/Shutterstock; 165 (UP RT), irin-k/Shutterstock; 165 (LO), Richard Peterson/Shutterstock; 166, Jonathan Halling; 167, Sodapix/PhotoLibrary; 167, Redmond Durrell/Alamy; 168-169, Eric Dietrich/Hedgehog House/Minden Pictures; 172, NOAA; 174-175, Danylchenko Iaroslav/Shutterstock; 176, Karine Aigner/NGS Staff; 176 (RT), Jim Barber/Shutterstock; 179 (UP), Mark Williams/National Geographic Creative; 179 (LO), Jonathan Halling; 180-181, Michael Freeman/Aurora Photos; 182, Jonathan Halling; 184, Ingram Publishing/SuperStock; 185, Chris Moore; 186-187, Sam Abell/National Geographic Creative; 186, Todd Pussler/npl/Minden Pictures; 188, Jonathan Halling; 189, The Royal Collection © 2008, Her Majesty Queen Elizabeth II; 190, Pixeldust Studios; 192-193, Karen Kasmauski/National Geographic Creative; 196, Lori Epstein; 197, Juniors Bildarchiv/Photolibrary; 198, Daniel Hubert/National Geographic Creative; 201, Creatas/PhotoLibrary; 203, SuperStock RF/SuperStock; 207, Jonathan Halling

215

Copyright © 2010 National Geographic Society
Copyright © 2018 National Geographic
Partners, LLC

Since 1888, the National Geographic Society has
funded more than 12,000 research, exploration,
and preservation projects around the world.
The Society receives funds from National
Geographic Partners, LLC, funded in part by
your purchase. A portion of the proceeds from
this book supports this vital work. To learn
more, visit natgeo.com/info.

For more information, visit
nationalgeographic.com, call 1-800-647-5463,
or write to the following address:

National Geographic Partners
1145 17th Street N.W.
Washington, D.C. 20036-4688 U.S.A.

Visit us online at nationalgeographic.com/books

For librarians and teachers:
ngchildrensbooks.org

More for kids from National Geographic:
natgeokids.com

For information about special discounts
for bulk purchases, please contact National
Geographic Books Special Sales:
specialsales@natgeo.com

For rights or permissions inquiries, please
contact National Geographic Books Subsidiary
Rights: bookrights@natgeo.com

Designed by Rachael Hamm Plett, Moduza Design

First edition published 2010
Reissued and updated 2018

Trade paperback: 978-1-4263-3106-0
Reinforced library binding ISBN:
978-1-4263-3107-7

The publisher would like to thank Jen
Agresta, project manager; Sharon Thompson,
researcher; Kelsey Turek, researcher; Michelle
Harris, researcher; Robin Terry, project
editor; Paige Towler, project editor; Eva
Absher-Schantz, art director; Julide Dengel,
art director; Kathryn Robbins, art director;
Ruthie Thompson, designer; Lori Epstein, photo
director; Jay Sumner, photo editor; Hillary Leo,
photo editor; Alix Inchausti, production editor;
and Anne LeongSon and Gus Tello, production
assistants.

Printed in China
18/PPS/1

BABY HEDGEHOGS are called ~~~~ ~~~~ ANIMALS,
HOGLET~~ ~~~~ACES,
~~CRAZY INVENTIONS,~~
FREAKY PHENOMENA,
ASTONISHING FEATS,
and more with fun and
funny facts and photos
about our **wacky world!**

weird but true! 1 — 350 OUTRAGEOUS FACTS
weird but true! 2 — 350 OUTRAGEOUS FACTS
weird but true! 3 — 350 OUTRAGEOUS FACTS
weird but true! 4 — 350 OUTRAGEOUS FACTS
weird but true! 5 — 350 OUTRAGEOUS FACTS
weird but true! 6 — 350 OUTRAGEOUS FACTS
weird but true! 7 — 350 OUTRAGEOUS FACTS
weird but true! 8 — 350 OUTRAGEOUS FACTS
weird but true! 9 — 350 OUTRAGEOUS FACTS
weird but true! 10 — 350 OUTRAGEOUS FACTS

Available Wherever Books Are Sold!

natgeokids.com

$8.99 U.S. / $11.99 CAN / £6.99 UK
ISBN 978-1-4263-3106-0 /Printed in China

Collect All 10!